ACTION SPORTS

SKATEBOARDING

KENNY ABDO

abdopublishing.com

Published by Abdo Zoom, a division of ABDO, P.O. Box 398166, Minneapolis, Minnesota 55439. Copyright © 2018 by Abdo Consulting Group, Inc. International copyrights reserved in all countries. No part of this book may be reproduced in any form without written permission from the publisher.

Printed in the United States of America, North Mankato, Minnesota.
092017
012018

THIS BOOK CONTAINS
RECYCLED MATERIALS

Photo Credits: AP Images, Getty Images, GraphicStock, iStock, Shutterstock
Production Contributors: Kenny Abdo, Jennie Forsberg, Grace Hansen
Design Contributors: Dorothy Toth, Neil Klinepier

Publisher's Cataloging-in-Publication Data

Names: Abdo, Kenny, author.
Title: Skateboarding / by Kenny Abdo.
Description: Minneapolis, Minnesota: Abdo Zoom, 2018. | Series: Action sports |
     Includes online resource and index.
Identifiers: LCCN 2017939272 | ISBN 9781532120947 (lib.bdg.) |
     ISBN 9781532122064 (ebook) | ISBN 9781532122620 (Read-to-Me ebook)
Subjects: LCSH: Skateboarding--Juvenile literature. | Extreme Sports--
     Juvenile literature.
Classification: DDC 796.22--dc23
LC record available at https://lccn.loc.gov/2017939272

TABLE OF CONTENTS

SKATEBOARDING

Skateboarding is a sport that involves riding and performing tricks on a small board attached to wheels.

Skateboarding was created from surfing and was initially known as sidewalk surfing. The first skateboard was introduced in 1950.

TYPES

Skateboards consist of three parts: the **deck**, the **trucks** and the wheels.

TRUCK

WHEEL

DECK

9

Early boards used wheels made of metal or clay. These were slow, noisy and clumsy. In the 1970s, polyurethane wheels came onto the market.

Skateboarders used to practice in empty swimming pools. Later they began to use **ramps**. Advanced skateboarders use a **half pipe**.

There are many types of competitive skateboarding. Some include freestyle, **vert**, street, and big air.

Tony Hawk was the first to land the difficult trick, the 900. He spun his skateboard two and a half times in mid-air before landing at the 1999 X-Games.

Three of the most important skateboarding tricks are the **kickturn**, the **ollie**, and the **grind**.

Skateboarding has made its mark among the top ten most popular sports in the world.

GLOSSARY

deck – the wooden board skaters ride on.

grind – riding the trucks or board against a rail or curb.

half pipe – a ramp with two sloped sides between a flat section.

kickturn – swinging the front of the deck to a new direction.

ollie – a basic trick where a rider leaps the skateboard into the air.

ramp – a platform that allows skaters to get air.

trucks – two aluminum pieces that attach wheels to the deck.

vert – riding from the ground to a ramp to perform tricks.

ONLINE RESOURCES

Booklinks
NONFICTION NETWORK
FREE! ONLINE NONFICTION RESOURCES

To learn more about skateboarding, please visit abdobooklinks.com. These links are routinely monitored and updated to provide the most current information available.

INDEX